Keith Reddin

Rum and Coke

D0822440

357 W 20th St., NY NY 10011
212 627-1055

RUM AND COKE
© Copyright 1986 by Keith Reddin

First printing: September 1986
Second printing: April 1990
ISBN: 0-88145-042-1

Cover Art by Paul Davis Studio
Design by Marie Donovan
Set in Aster by L&F Technical Composition, Lakeland, FL
Printed on acid-free paper and bound in the USA.

For

Howard Barker

Rum and Coke was presented by the New York Shakespeare Festival on January 27, 1986 with Joseph Papp, producer, and Jason Steven Cohen, associate producer.

The play was directed by Les Waters. Scenery by John Arnone. Costumes by Kurt Wilhelm. Lighting by Stephen Strawbridge. Projections by Wendall Harrington. Production Stage Manager was Janet P. Callahan. Stage Manager, David Lansky. The cast was as follows:

JAKE SEWARD	Peter MacNicol
RODGER POTTER	Michael Ayr
TOD CARTMELL	John Bedford-Lloyd
BAR PATRON	Frank Maraden
BAR WAITER	Jose Ramon Rosario
LINDA SEWARD	Polly Draper
THOMAS TANNER	Larry Bryggman
BOB STANTON	Robert Stanton
JORGE	Jose Fong
MIGUEL	Tony Plana
RICHARD M. NIXON	Frank Maraden
FELIX DUQUE	Jose Ramon Rosario
CHILD #1	Jose Fong
CHILD #2	Robert Stanton
COMMANDER TYLER	John Bedford-Lloyd
RAMON	Michael Ayr
RAMON'S GRANDMOTHER	Frank Maraden
LARRY PETERS	Larry Bryggman
FIDEL CASTRO	John Bedford-Lloyd

Rum and Coke was presented in an earlier version at the Yale Repertory 5th Annual Winterfest of New Works. Bill Partlan directed.

The world premiere was presented at the South Coast Repertory Theatre. David Emmes directed.

Author's Note

Many people were involved in the shaping of *Rum and Coke* and I would like to thank them for their support and insight:

Joel Schechter and Adam Versenyi from the Yale Repertory Theatre, Jerry Patch and John Glore from South Coast Repertory Theatre, Gail Merrifield, Bill Hart and Morgan Jenness from the Public Theatre Literary staff, Les Waters, the director of the Public Theatre production, and especially Joseph Papp, for his wonderful help and encouragement.

Order of Scenes

Act One

Act Two

ACT ONE

Prologue

(Lights on JAKE)

JAKE: The few memories I have of actually being in Cuba come from my sister. She remembers riding a horse through sugar cane fields, the plants so high you couldn't see the horse in front of you.

She remembers a night in the Tropicana, when a gangster from Terre Haute lost 47,000 on one roll of the dice while she sat drinking Cuba Libra, Free Cuba, what they call Rum and Coke.

She talked of a boy who fell in love with her and for a year afterwards wrote her passionate letters expressing his love, devotion, and a burning desire to come to America to study medicine at Columbia.

I remember a black-and-white snapshot of my sister in a swimsuit holding hands with a kid in white shorts and black knee socks and saddle shoes. The kid is me. The back of the snapshot says "Havana, April, 1939."

This is a bar in Miami, 1960. It's called Barry's Luau, and is conveniently located off Runway Nine, Miami International Airport. Meeting me are a guy I knew worked with the Agency in Guatemala. The other guy was a big-shot businessman, Tod Cartmell, affectionately known as Shit Pickle Cartmell.

And this is how I got messed up in something called the Bay of Pigs.

Scene Two

(Lights up on the bar. Jukebox in corner plays Sinatra singing "Come Fly With Me." RODGER at table, JAKE joins him. CARTMELL upstage.)

RODGER: Mr. Cartmell is like a number of people concerned about what is currently happening in our sphere of influence. We have a Communist government, ruled by Russia, ninety miles from the Florida keys. They're building up their armies, they are receiving shipments of arms from the Soviets, and there is the threat of the exportation of Soviet Marxist-Leninism at our back door. Think about that. Ninety miles. Eight jet minutes from Florida.

CARTMELL: What you guys wanna hear?

JAKE: Sinatra's fine.

CARTMELL: Great. The Chairman of the Board. I'm thinking about buying me this juke.

RODGER: It's a threat to our security and our way of life. The Russians understand this, they do. Mr. Kruschev doesn't like it but he understands how the game is played. Containment, Jake. The policy is vigilance and containment. You look good, Jake. Healthy.

JAKE: You sit in the sun awhile, you look good.

CARTMELL: *(Coming over to table)* This colored woman I talk to she tells me, eat a mess of dirt every day, it'll keep you healthy.

JAKE: I've never heard that.

CARTMELL: Got relatives in Corn Cob, Georgia, someplace, send her north a shoebox of black dirt from home. This woman, she sprinkle a little water on it, makes it muddy, you know, she smiling, eating this dirt. Keep me healthy, get my strength up, Mr. Cartmell. That's what she says to me. Get my strength up. One day, she looking low, I says Dorothy, how come you look like shit, I kid her, see? I can say she look like shit somedays, she don't mind, she says "Oh Mr. Cartmell, I'm outta dirt, good rich Georgia dirt, black soil, that's why I'm feeling so poorly." She tells me eating dirt makes her grandmother live to be a hundred and five, don't that beat all? Huh? What are you boys drinking?

RODGER: I'm just drinking beer, Mr. Cartmell.

CARTMELL: Have yourself a Jack Daniels.

RODGER: Mr. Cartmell...

CARTMELL: What's this "Mr. Cartmell" crap?

RODGER: Tod, Shit Pickle here, is a wealthy individual...

CARTMELL: So they tell me.

RODGER: ... who is as concerned as we are...

CARTMELL: Didn't get rich from eating DIRT, I can tell you.

JAKE: I can see.

CARTMELL: See, I've know old Roge here awhile. Knew him when he was working with United Fruit. You've heard of United Fruit, right?

JAKE: Sure.

CARTMELL: Rodger here, he's a good man. Everybody over at United Fruit real happy with his work, am I right?

RODGER: No complaints, Tod.

CARTMELL: Rodger, who is a good buddy, a good worker, he said he was talking to you. I thought we should get together, have a talk. Have some fun. Now we're having some fun.

JAKE: Yes, we are.

CARTMELL: See, we were talking about Cuba...

RODGER: About Castro...

CARTMELL: People who, God forbid, have been forced to flee their own fucking homeland.

JAKE: Uh-huh.

CARTMELL: You want another beer, Rodger?

RODGER: I'm fine, Tod.

CARTMELL: Jake?

JAKE: Sure.

CARTMELL: Another round!

RODGER: We are thinking at this point of capitalizing on the vast Cuban underground and organizing a typical Latin upheaval, sort of Guatemalan scenario.

CARTMELL: We kicked ass down there with only 150 men.

JAKE: What can I do for you, Rodger?

CARTMELL: Hey, where are those drinks?

RODGER: We're aware of that radio campaign you did for our embassy down in Venezuela.

JAKE: Campaign, I just played records and made jokes about the Venezuelan president.

RODGER: Jake, that was very effective.

JAKE: Really? ... Thanks.

CARTMELL: Jake, you swim?

JAKE: Sure, sometimes.

CARTMELL: Health is very important

RODGER: Tod here is interested in health.

CARTMELL: This guy I got, works on my lawn, okay, I call him a gardener, he mows the grass, he's a healthy guy, big. He comes up to me one day, he says, Mr. Cartmell, I feel terrible all the time lately. You been

eating Dorothy's dirt, I say? (*Laughs*) No, just kidding.
Well listen here Walter, I say. Walter, you get yourself
to a doctor, you find out what the HELL is wrong with
you. Doctor says a tape worm. A big old worm inside of
his stomach. Well, I looked him over, he didn't look
wormy or nothing, but he looked green as shit. I said,
Walter, what you going to do? He says doctor give me
some drugs to flush this worm out of my system, and
he says I gotta sit with my ass over a bowl of milk,
cause that attracts this worm out. So later on he's telling me how he's watching T.V. or something, his pants
around his ankles, heaving and pushing, and feel this
worm come outta his ass. This worm the size of an
orange comes outta his ass, plop, into this bowl of milk
he's squatting over. And he takes this worm all rolled
up, takes it to the doctor. The doctor unravels this
worm, it was maybe four, five feet long, when the doctor stretched it out, but see—(*Giggling*) see, this doctor,
he turns to Walter and says this worm ain't got a head.
(*Laughs*) Get it? While he was passing the worm the old
sphincter cuts off the worm at its head—(*Giggles*) see,
worms they can regenerate from the head. Your health
is important. You got your health you do all right. You
boys hungry? You want something to eat?

JAKE: Oh, no thanks.

CARTMELL: Well, time to put another nickle in, in the
nickelodeon. Hey, Rodger-dodger.

(TOD *walks over to jukebox, puts money in. Sinatra
singing* "South of the Border".)

RODGER: Jake, you follow me so far? We want you to
handle the radio operations, train these Cubans in
broadcasting, teach them to do what you do so well.

JAKE: What, play records and make political jokes?

RODGER: Yeah, and the Agency's got some ideas.

CARTMELL: (*Back at the table.*) "South of the Border,"
huh? Get it, huh?

(*A* PATRON *comes over to the table.*)

PATRON: You guys playing the jukebox?

CARTMELL: Who wants to know?

PATRON: You the pecker head who keeps playing Sinatra?

CARTMELL: What did you say, buster?

PATRON: I said I'm tired of hearing Sinatra playing in this place. I'm having a drink, talking to my girl-friend, I don't wanna hear no more Sinatra.

JAKE: Sorry.

CARTMELL: You don't like this song?

PATRON: Listen weasel, I don't like this song, I don't like Sinatra, I don't like your face.

CARTMELL: You're upsetting me now, fellow.

RODGER: Sit down, Tod, the man is drunk.

CARTMELL: I think you should shut up and get out.

PATRON: I think Sinatra can't sing dick. He should fuck a dead cat and he'd still sound the same.

RODGER: The man's an asshole, Tod.

CARTMELL: Everyone is entitled to his opinion but you don't happen to know shit. (*He kicks* PATRON *in the groin.*) You hear this turkey? You hear what he said about Frank Sinatra? I don't believe these people.

JAKE: Mr. Cartmell, take it easy, the guy was drunk.

CARTMELL: (*Throwing money at them.*) You remember something, Joe College. People like me pay your sal-aries. We keep this country going. Rodger, if you wanna talk to me I'll be over at the Kenilworth, got a couple of girls coming over tonight. But first, I'm gonna have that dumb fuck's legs broken.

(WAITER *comes over with tray of drinks.*)

Now you come, you stupid fuck, we don't want the drinks now. I'm surrounded by incompetence.

(CARTMELL *exits*, WAITER *helps* PATRON *off*.)

JAKE: People like him used to run fraternities.

RODGER: Tod, Mr. Cartmell, had a large interest in several Havana hotels and casinos before the revolution. People like Cartmell are an unfortunate aspect of our work, but they do not represent central intelligence. Cartmell, and Cartmell Construction can hook us up with the right people in Guatemala, get us a place for training the rebels. But remember. We're the hope, Jake. You and me, a new generation of go-getters, Americans. This country gave for us, now it's our turn. To give. To sacrifice. To be an American.

JAKE: I understand.

RODGER: I'm talking about ninety miles from here, Jake. I'm not waving flags here, I'm talking about common sense. It's got to be stopped now. We can do that.

JAKE: Well, it's a challenging opportunity. I'll think about it, Rodger, and I'll let you know.

RODGER: Sorry about the evening turning out this way.

(*They shake hands.* RODGER *exits.*)

Scene Three

(*Lights up on* JAKE *and* LINDA *in deck chairs.* JAKE *wears his suit and sunglasses.* LINDA *in a black swimsuit and sunglasses.*)

LINDA: God, I love the sun, Jake. I could just sit here, by this pool, and just bake, like a goddamn bean, you know. (*Looks at* JAKE.) Really dressed for the beach, huh, Jake?

JAKE: Yeah.

LINDA: I could be like that French king, the one they called the Sun King, only I'd be the Sun Queen, that French king, Louis the whatever.

JAKE: The one with the furniture.

LINDA: (*Sarcastic*) That's the one.

JAKE: Like his chairs.

LINDA: Jake, fellah, aren't you a bit hot in those duds?

JAKE: I'm fine, Linda.

LINDA: Okay. How was Miami?

JAKE: That was fine.

LINDA: You look good. What happened?

JAKE: You swim, you stay healthy.

LINDA: You gonna stick around awhile?

JAKE: Going to be traveling soon.

LINDA: Oh? Where?

JAKE: South America, possibly. Panama, Guatemala, one of those countries where the lush flora and fauna meet the gleaming steel and glass of modern housing developments.

LINDA: I'm crazy about traveling.

JAKE: Lois Lane with a flight bag. See Lois partying with heads of state, see Lois at the duty free shop at the airport.

LINDA: It's not always that glamourous, Jake.

JAKE: Some assignments you actually work?

LINDA: I was in Russia. Stalking Vice-President Nixon. When we met Kruschev. The Kitchen Debates. You remember that?

JAKE: (*Singing*) Someone's in the kitchen with Kruschev. I vaguely remember that article.

LINDA: It was the cover story, Jake.

JAKE: Richard Nixon's a regular pal of mine.

LINDA: Uh huh.

JAKE: Told me he'd find me work someday. No, he just said thanks. I made that into someday he'll get me work, repay certain favors done.

LINDA: So what are you up to now?

JAKE: I think I'm going to do something for...

LINDA: For who?

JAKE: For God, for country, and for Yale.

LINDA: In that order?

JAKE: No, just the country part.

LINDA: Which country, Connecticut?

JAKE: No, Linda, I'm going to do something good. Something I think is good.

LINDA: You're serious.

JAKE: Yeah. I am. Serious. About doing something. And I feel like I been drifting along. Now, I'm going to do something. I mean, I'm here, right? I'm an American, right? I want to do something for America.

LINDA: What are you going to do, work for the government?

JAKE: Well, you work for goddamn Time-Life. That's the same as working for the government.

LINDA: Jake, I'm a journalist, I try to uncover what's going on ... to disseminate information.

JAKE: Within the confines of Time-Life and Henry Luce.

LINDA: That's a problem, okay, sure. But I'm out there Jake. I see the world, and I listen, and I ask questions. I get the truth heard and sometimes that scares people, the truth.

JAKE: (*Pause*) It's so damn hot out here.

LINDA: Jake, whatever it is you're going to do, just remember who pulls the strings. The guys up there.

JAKE: You ever think about why you can write the stuff you do? Cause those guys pullin' those strings believe in letting people write what they want. Think about that while you're sitting by a pool in some posh country club.

LINDA: You think about who you're working for and what they want in the end.

JAKE: I know, Linda. I know what they want and it's what I want. I am sweating so much.

LINDA: Hey, I'm sorry. I'm sorry I push you, Jake. I always push. You want to stay for lunch?

JAKE: No, I gotta go, Linda. Actually I do have to go.

LINDA: How's Mom?

JAKE: Fine. How's Dad?

LINDA: Fine.

JAKE: Fine. Dad's fine. We're all fine. (*Pause*) When you see him, tell him I'm ... just tell him hello for me ... I'll just take this weekly news magazine with me to read on the plane ... Be good.

LINDA: Page 37, Jake.

(*He exits. Lights fade.*)

Scene Four

(*Lights up on CIA office.*)

TANNER: Rodger, like you to meet Bob Stanton. And you are?

JAKE: Jake. Jake Seward. The operative in the propaganda unit. Training the rebels. In Guatemala.

TANNER: Right. Rodger, here, is my liaison man for Cuba. Now Bob was outlining various scenarios for the removal of Castro.

RODGER: Assassination?

TANNER: Possibly, but not necessarily.

BOB: We've been tossing around various proposals to undermine the viability of Castro as leader. Undermining his popular support.

RODGER: Uh huh.

TANNER: Bob talked with Technical Services Division...

BOB: You know Stuart Giles over at TSD?

RODGER: No, not personally.

BOB: Doesn't matter. Stuart's got this idea to spray the radio studio where Castro makes his broadcasts with LSD. Disorient the man, in no time at all, he starts babbling on the air, telling them to wear their underwear on their head, the people figure their Presidente has a few screws loose. Course we gotta get a contact into the studio itself, right before. Stuart thought Tom knew an operative.

TANNER: We have a possible operative who can hook up with Castro, but I can't confirm his availability.

RODGER: LSD is a rather unstable chemical.

TANNER: The Army has done tests.

RODGER: But those tests are inconclusive. Our operative runs the risk of being contaminated himself.

(*Pause*)

BOB: Put it in a box of those cigars he always smokes. He doesn't pass those around.

TANNER: Possible.

BOB: (*Opens file.*) I also have a report here on Thallium salts. Now we could get somebody to dust Fidel's shoes with this stuff. Thallium is a strong depilatory, could cause his beard to fall out overnight.

TANNER: We could wait till he's visiting some foreign country.

BOB: Or New York...

TANNER: Or New York addressing the U.N. And he's staying at some hotel...

BOB: Right.

TANNER: He leaves his shoes outside the room to get shined for the big speech...

BOB: We have an agent sprinkle this Thallium, his beard falls out, his image would be irredeemably damaged.

TANNER: Do we have a picture of what he looks like without a beard? Rodger? Do we have a picture in our files?

RODGER: I'm not sure.

TANNER: Check this out for me, will you?

RODGER: Right away sir.

TANNER: You following this, uh ... Wait. It'll come to me.

JAKE: The guy from the radio.

TANNER: Oh, Jake, Jake Seward, on the radio... Caracas. You were with Nixon in Caracas, am I correct?

JAKE: Yes sir.

TANNER: Nixon talks about that trip.

BOB: Yes, he does.

(*Pause*)

TANNER: I remember that period, very rocky. A period of choices. Well those choices are being made. Jake, you see this plate on my desk. It says "Be blunt, be brief, be gone."

JAKE: Absolutely.

BOB: Tom. Tell them about the time you walked right up to the president and said, "I'm you're man-eating shark."

TANNER: Bob, pass that box over here.

BOB: Right, Tom.

TANNER: This is a box of the same kind of cigars Fidel smokes. Had an operative send them to me. Go ahead, Rodger, Jake.

RODGER: Well...

TANNER: Go ahead. You too, Bob.

BOB: Thank you, Tom.

(*All four take a cigar, light up as they continue talking.*)

TANNER: Rodger, you been out on my sloop, I take you out on the Marcus Aurelius?

RODGER: Not yet.

TANNER: Remind me to take you out one weekend.

RODGER: All right.

TANNER: Bob's been out.

BOB: Yes, yes, I have. It was a wonderful weekend, Tom ... Tom got caught in this freak storm...

TANNER: It just came up, sky darkened, winds came up, twelve-foot swells, zero visibility, but I got us back.

BOB: Quite a skipper. Got us out of that squall.

JAKE: Uh, sir...

TANNER: What?

JAKE: These cigars...

TANNER: What?

(*Pause*)

JAKE: They haven't...

TANNER: What?

JAKE: They haven't been ... they're not ... I mean I feel a little lightheaded.

TANNER: Yes?

(*Pause*)

JAKE: They haven't been tampered with?

BOB: What, these cigars treated?

TANNER: Jake, I wouldn't give you, Rodger, Bob, and myself chemically imbalanced cigars, that's ridiculous.

BOB: Yes sir.

TANNER: You don't smoke cigars often, do you, Jake?

JAKE: No.

TANNER: Well, there you are then. Bob, what else you got?

BOB: Castro could be eliminated by the Cuban underground. But not someone in the exile rebel forces, that could tie them to us. We couldn't have this guy caught and tell them we paid him to terminate Castro. We were thinking about using the mob.

TANNER: The underworld crime families.

BOB: Yes. We contact FBI and they put us on some mob people, who for the right price, could cause an accident to neutralize Castro. For the money they ask, within reason, of course, they could do the job.

TANNER: What are we talking about?

BOB: The price floating around is a hundred, a hundred-fifty thousand.

TANNER: To get rid of Castro.

BOB: It could be done, and it would not come back to us.

RODGER: Are these people approachable, would they do business with us?

BOB: You have to remember that a great deal of syndicate money was tied up in the Cuban nightclub and casino industry. The various drug traffic and prostitution organizations were being fed by underworld money. It seems to me that they would jump at the chance to pay Mr. Fidel back for this nationalizing of industry.

TANNER: Thank you, Bob. (*To* JAKE) You ever play with trains? Toy trains?

JAKE: Sir?

TANNER: My grandfather was the president of a railroad. I studied train schedules and routes; often I would mentally reroute systems or build new systems where one did not exist. For example, on the Union Pacific main line, west of Cheyenne I discovered a stretch of about a hundred miles that had been built in the wrong place. If the railroads had followed the North Platte, they could have circumvented Sherman Hill, lowered their highest grade by five hundred to a thousand feet, and made the trip more efficient. This kind of oversight does not merely annoy me, Jake. It offends. Have fun in Guatemala.

(*Lights dim.*)

Scene Five

(*Sound of pouring rain.* JAKE, *very wet, standing in mess tent with* MIGUEL *and* GEORGE, *two Cuban rebels.*)

JAKE: Does it always rain this much here?

GEORGE: Very much rain.

JAKE: Great. Ten days in glorious Guatemala and I haven't seen the sun. Miguel, where are the others?

MIGUEL: They are seeing the movie *Where the Boys Are* with Tab Hunter and Paula Prentiss.

JAKE: Yes, I know the film. Why don't we pick up where we left off. When transmitting the propaganda, first we ask for the grass roots support. That is the men, women and children in the villages, the farms, work on the families that have reason to distrust the regime, Castro has promised, but he hasn't delivered. Jorge for example.

GEORGE: Castro said he would educate the people.

JAKE: Well, Jorge, that's not a good example because he has begun improving the literacy rate in Cuba.

MIGUEL: Yes, he does that.

JAKE: I know he does that. That's not a good example because guys, that's something he promised and he's doing it, so that won't make people rise up against him, and so that won't help when we hit the beaches. Well, when you guys hit the beaches.

MIGUEL: Castro have many corrupt people around him. People take money like in Batista.

JAKE: Good, good talk about how Castro promised to clean things up, but actually nothing has changed. In fact, say things have gotten worse. Something like: Castro, who has promised so much, Fidel who you all welcomed with open arms, Fidel who has used us, has trapped us, who is controlled by the fools, the traitors, the self-servers, the ass-lickers, the power hungry, the sexual deviants ... then go straight from sexual deviants to communists. Castro has betrayed us by becoming a Soviet puppet. Fidel the traitor selling us for the Soviet ruble. Hit them with Soviet oppression leads to Cuban oppression.

GEORGE: He sells Cuba out.

MIGUEL: He is a communist.

JAKE: Right.

MIGUEL: He is a communist sexual deviant.

JAKE: We don't need to put them in the same sentence, Miguel. Okay, name the cast of the *Nun's Story*, Warner Brothers, 1959.

GEORGE: Audrey Hepburn, Edith Evans, Rosalie Gruthley, Dean Jager, Stephen Murphy, and Peter Finch as the attractive but agnostic physician she meets in the Congo.

JAKE: Very good. Okay Miguel, the movie is *Up Periscope*.

MIGUEL: Uh, Edmond O'Brien, Alan Hale, and Carleton Carpenter.

GEORGE: You left out James Garner.

JAKE: You forgot James Garner, Miguel, but it was a good try. Next week I think they're showing more movies because I'm sure it will still be raining, so study those credits carefully.

MIGUEL: Will it be another movie about oral hygiene?

JAKE: God, I hope not. Now let's get back to work ... Castro does not allow any free expression, Cuba is becoming a totalitarian prison where all liberties are oppressed...

(*Sound of helicopter landing.*)

Listen, we'll have to continue this later. I've gotta talk to my boss from the Agency.

MIGUEL: From Washington

JAKE: Yeah. Don't worry. I'll talk to him about ... the problem.

MIGUEL: Good. We can see the end of *Where the Boys Are.*

(JAKE *and* MIGUEL *exit.*)

(RODGER *enters, walks over to* JAKE.)

JAKE: In here, Rodger. Welcome to Guatemala.

RODGER: Beautiful country here. Nice mountain.

JAKE: It's volcano, Rodger. They set this camp up next to an active volcano. I got here, the only thing the government supplied was the refrigerator. To keep the beer cold for the rebels.

RODGER: Uh huh.

JAKE: There's poisonous snakes, no medical supplies, no showers, the mosquitos are terrible, and I haven't had a chance to work on my tan. But you know, Rodger, the thing is these guys listen to me. They really listen. I get them together and they are so respectful and ... they hang on my every word. They write down everything I say, and they seem really eager to learn, to advance and I guess ... that's great, Rodger. They make me feel we're moving ahead.

RODGER: So, what's your problem, Jake?

JAKE: We've had some complaints from the President of Guatemala.

RODGER: Doesn't the President like the Americans in his country?

JAKE: He likes us, especially the money, fine. It's the Cubans I'm training he's not crazy about.

RODGER: What's the matter with the Cubans?

JAKE: They want to get laid.

RODGER: Understandable.

JAKE: But where we gonna find women to service a brigade of horny freedom fighters in the middle of some Central American jungle? The President is greatly distressed by the reports he receives of the Cuban freedom fighters sneaking out at night and recking havoc with the local women. So the government of the United States is going to have to supply prostitutes to the government of Guatemala to then service the Cuban invasion force.

RODGER: I'll get you the official okay.

JAKE: Just get us the whores. The guys here are so hot for Kim Novak we had to show Pal Joey seven times this week.

RODGER: Don't worry. I'll get you the whores. Damn. Money is going to be a problem. We're already $400 overbudget on the airstrip down here. It's possible we could print up coupons for the men. Let the rebels go for free, but charge the locals. Maybe even turn a profit. You know it might work.

JAKE: Please. Whatever it takes. Maybe I'll see you next week in the States.

RODGER: You have a bricfing?

JAKE: No, a lunch date. Rodger. Did you bring...?

RODGER: (*Handing roll of toilet paper.*) Oh, sure.

JAKE: Thank you, Rodger.

(*Lights dim.*)

Scene Six

(*Lights up on the Oyster Bar, Grand Central Station.*)

LINDA: You're late.

JAKE: You were probably early.

LINDA: Where did you get that jacket?

JAKE: Mother picked it out. She saw this jacket in some catalog. She knew I weigh the same since high school. She sent it to me.

LINDA: I hope you don't go around telling people that your mother still buys your clothes.

JAKE: Hell no, it would spoil my image.

LINDA: As what?

JAKE: As ... I don't know ... a man of the world.

LINDA: Do you still wear white socks with your suits?

(JAKE *tries to hid his socks.*)

JAKE: How's Time-Life?

LINDA: Oh, oodles of fun. Had lunch with Jackie Kennedy. Senator Kennedy's wife.

JAKE: I know who Jackie Kennedy is. I read your magazine.

LINDA: Not mine.

JAKE: Mr. Luce's magazine.

LINDA: Mr. Luce wouldn't like to hear you call it my magazine. Although I like to think so.

JAKE: How is Jackie?

LINDA: Gave me the scoop Jack's gonna be the next president.

JAKE: How's she know?

LINDA: Jack told her he was.

JAKE: How's Jack know?

LINDA: His father said he would be.

JAKE: Really.

LINDA: Just kidding.

JAKE: He wasn't.

LINDA: Probably not. Jackie'll make a good first lady. She's got more class than Mamie Eisenhower.

JAKE: I have more class than Mamie Eisenhower.

LINDA: Jackie told me she took a tour of the White House the other day, strictly tourist scene with a bunch of other Senator's wives.

JAKE: She was probably deciding how she was gonna re-decorate.

LINDA: Who told?

JAKE: Go on.

LINDA: She told me how the floors, these beautiful polished wood floors are ripped to shit because Ike walks around in his golf shoes. The man walks around in cleats swinging a nine iron. What a joke.

JAKE: You're tough, Linda. You always were. Kids on the block used to tell me how tough you were. You know why we like Linda so much, they'd say? Because you can push her down and she won't cry or nothing. You can push her down and she'll get right back up and push you down.

LINDA: I did that.

JAKE: I know you did. You used to push me down.

LINDA: You hated having an older sister.

JAKE: I thought you were my older brother. You could climb a tree as good as anyone. Dad would take you hunting. Dad would teach you how to drive. Dad'd teach you how to drink.

LINDA: Dad taught everybody how to drink.

JAKE: Sure. Mom would pick out my clothes, Dad and you would be hunting quail or something.

LINDA: You working for the CIA or what?

JAKE: How about those Yankees, Linda? Think they'll win the pennant?

LINDA: Answer me.

JAKE: Sure I'm working for the CIA.

LINDA: Jake, aren't you going to lie at least? Aren't you going to deny it, give me some cover?

JAKE: Why? You'd figure it out soon enough. You know everything. So you always tell me.

LINDA: I just heard you were working for the Agency.

JAKE: You want a lie or what?

LINDA: You are, aren't you?

JAKE: No, I sell greeting cards, Linda. You know that.

LINDA: Why are you working for those people?

JAKE: I sell novelty items in Central America.

LINDA: Jake...

JAKE: Whoopie cushions, slinky glasses, and ever-famous dribble glass...

LINDA: Jake, how on Earth did you get involved with these people?

JAKE: Well, I think Richard Nixon put in a good word for me.

LINDA: Richard Nixon, the Vice-President?

JAKE: No, Richard Nixon the caterer. Of course, the Vice-President. Yeah, I was in Venezuela, working at the Embassy...

LINDA: The job Dad set up for you...

JAKE: Whatever, so listen, anyway, I'm down there being junior attaché in South America and there's old Dick on his good-will tour of our neighbors south of the border...

Scene Seven

(*On empty stage large black limo pulls on. Pause. Then car is pelted with eggs for about ten seconds. Shouts. Pause. Slowly car doors start to open. More eggs pelt the car, the doors quickly close. Pause. JAKE enters from the side, knocks on back door. Shouts off-stage. Door opens. JAKE talks into back of car through door.*)

JAKE: Over here, sir. Welcome to Caracas, Mr. Vice-President.

(*Slowly NIXON exits car, looks around.*)

NIXON: Is that a mob over there?

JAKE: Yes, sir. I'm with the American Embassy here. My name is Jake Seward.

NIXON: Nice to meet you, Jake. What are they shouting?

JAKE: Roughly it translates Death to Nixon.

NIXON: Oh.

JAKE: Also, Death to United States. Death to Imperialist Aggressors, that kind of thing.

NIXON: Right.

JAKE: It is my responsibility not to allow any harm to come to you while you're here, not that there's going to be a problem.

NIXON: Jake, I was warned of anti-American mobs. I was informed of hostile Communist groups ready to riot and create incident. But let me explain something here, Jake.

JAKE: Go ahead, sir.

NIXON: Jake, my advisors advised me against this Caracas visit. But once I had made this decision as a representative of American interests, in the interest of American foreign policy, at the request of our President, Dwight David Eisenhower, it is incumbent upon me, as that representative, to put aside those considerations, considerations of personal safety, and follow through. Because then it's not just a case of Richard Nixon being bluffed by a group of students, but of the United States putting its tail between its legs and running away from a bunch of communist thugs.

JAKE: Why didn't the President come, sir?

NIXON: He's the President, I'm the Vice-President. I make the trips, I go to the state funerals, I go to the summit conferences, I do the campaigning in the off-year elections, you know. Jake, you're new at this and so you don't know the territory. This is worse than the Republican National Convention.

JAKE: It's this heat south of the border, sir. This Latin humidity, you know? Makes everybody tense, everybody's got to shout.

NIXON: Right.

JAKE: These people, sir, the students, they don't understand Americans. They don't understand our policy, and you are a symbol of that policy. But they're just a small group, worked up and confused and...

(*Louder crowd noise.*)

They look kinda angry, sir.

NIXON: Jake, let me tell you something. I'm scared. All right? Maybe you don't know it, but I sweat, I sweat a lot. Christ, I think about a problem, and I get tense and I start sweating and then I go and stink, I

get so damned embarrassed I want to go hide.
Sometimes I get so damned scared of pissing people
off. People don't take to me, Jake. I am not the life of
the party, I can't tell jokes, I'm plain boring a lot of
the time. But I love this country.

JAKE: This country?

NIXON: The United States. America. I started out with
nothing, Jake, and now I'm a heartbeat away from being President, as they say. And that'll scare the shit out
of anybody, Jake. Think about that, Jake. Think about
that and sweating and having to shave twice a day so
you don't look like some hoodlum just walked off the
boat and Jake, I wish I wasn't here. I wish I was home
watching Uncle Milty or Robert Young and feeling
safe, and now you tell me there's a crowd of Commies
shouting Death to Nixon. Christ, I'm sweating.

JAKE: I'm sweating too, sir. But I want you to know
that it's an honor to be here with you.

NIXON: Fighting Communism is a bitch, you know?

JAKE: I bet. But once they see democracy in action
they'll know they're on the wrong track. They like to
make a lot of noise.

NIXON: Well, just keep smiling. That's all we can do,
Jake. Smile and talk to them and hope they'll listen.
They never do, but I never stop hoping.

JAKE: What was that?

NIXON: A rock.

JAKE: A rock?!

NIXON: Well, Jake, they're throwing rocks at us. Jake,
I think you should ride downtown with us.

JAKE: Let's get the hell out of here, Sir.

NIXON: When are these Latins gonna understand
we're here to help them, get their governments in
order, all we ask is to boot out the Communists.

JAKE: Sir, why don't you ... (*A rock hits* JAKE *in the face.*) Oh, shit. Shit fuck.

NIXON: What happened?

JAKE: I'm bleeding, feels like my nose ... oh, shit.

NIXON: Jake, you saved my life; get in the car, we'll get out of here.

JAKE: Goddamn stupid, don't they understand ... GODDAMNIT, I GRADUATED FROM YALE AND PEOPLE ARE TRYING TO KILL ME. JESUS CHRIST, WHAT AM I DOING HERE?

NIXON: It's all right, calm down, Jake.

JAKE: MY FATHER GOT ME A JOB IN THIS STUPID FUCKING EMBASSY. HE THOUGHT TRAVEL WOULD BE GOOD FOR ME. SHIT, SHIT A ROCK HIT MY FACE.

NIXON: Jake, jump in the car. I'll get you to a hospital.

JAKE: What's wrong with these people?!

NIXON: WILL YOU OPEN THE DOOR. What is the matter with these drivers? The man is bleeding here, we have to get out of this crowd of nuts and get to a hospital. (*He looks out.*) Jesus, they scare me.

(*Lights fade down on this scene.*)

Scene Eight

(*Lights up on* JAKE *and* LINDA *in Oyster Bar.*)

LINDA: I had no idea things were so wild down in Venezuela.

JAKE: Yeah, that trip really opened my eyes.

LINDA: (*Looking closely at him.*) Your nose doesn't look any different.

JAKE: Just a flesh wound, Linda.

LINDA: So now you're working for the CIA.

JAKE: I'm not at liberty to discuss this.

LINDA: Tell me about it.

JAKE: About what?

LINDA: About what you're working on.

JAKE: What, and read about it in *Time* magazine? I'm not that crazy.

LINDA: We know anyway.

JAKE: Then why do you ask?

LINDA: I thought you could give me confirmation. Tell me about Cuba.

JAKE: We're having lunch.

LINDA: Come on, Jake, talk.

JAKE: I don't want a press conference. I'm asking how you are. We talk about family, you ask about mother, I ask about Dad, I let you pay the bill.

LINDA: Jake, everybody knows.

JAKE: Fine, then I don't need to say anything.

LINDA: I mean I read about what's going on in the goddamn *New York Times*.

JAKE: Then you print the story in *Time* as yours, am I right?

LINDA: You people are doing this so clumsily, it's embarrassing.

JAKE: Linda...

LINDA: Nobody believes that these...

JAKE: What?

LINDA: That these so called rebels, these freedom fighters, just happened to get together on a whim.

Nobody in their right mind believes that these people, being armed and trained by the United States government, dropped supplies by United States Air Force, nobody believes that this is just some home grown Cuban counter-revolution. Jesus, can't you see the truth when it hits you in the face.

JAKE: Would you speak into the microphone, Linda, I'm not sure they're hearing you in distant galaxies.

LINDA: It is illegal and immoral.

JAKE: Illegal very possibly. Immoral, who is to say what is immoral in foreign policy?

(*Waiter enters, delivers the check. Exits.*)

LINDA: Jake, you ever hear anything you want me to know, you call me. You tell me about it. If enough people know, if enough people are embarrassed or compromised, maybe we could stop it.

JAKE: Maybe you could stop it, you mean. You want a piece of the action, you want the scoop.

LINDA: Maybe I see down the road, and maybe I understand what a colossal mistake it is. Cuba and all that.

JAKE: You want to be *Times's* man of the year, is that it? You itching to be editor-in-chief or work in the White House?

LINDA: Jake, you're full of shit and you know it. (*Pause*)

JAKE: You still remember Ramon, whatever his name is?

LINDA: Who?

JAKE: The Cuban medical student. The guy who was burning with desire for you.

LINDA: Of course I remember him. I remember Cuba, Jake. I remember when we were there, you were too young.

JAKE: We met some very nice people. It was a very nice place to live, I thought.

LINDA: If you had the money.

JAKE: I suppose.

LINDA: That's why they had a revolution.

(*Lights dim.*)

Scene Nine

(MIGUEL *at table*.)

MIGUEL: Lovers of freedom. Now is the hour of liberation. Now is the moment of decision. Today is the day when the clouds break and the sun of glory shines on us all. Take up your positions in the fields, in the roads, in the cities, in your homes. Down with the Soviet puppet Fidel Castro and his Soviet puppet regime. Down the oppression and mass arrest, down with censorship, and down with poverty, let us together take up arms and end the puppet government of Fidel Castro. Control roads and factories. Make prisoners and shoot those who refuse your orders. Jesus Christ and his saints look on this holy mission of liberation. The Virgin Mary and the angels shine on our efforts to free Cuba. Cuba Libra, friends. America is with you on this holy holy quest. The virgin prays for your success. One day soon, troops of rebels, rebels in the hills, rebels from the skies, rebels from the sea, will liberate you. They will ask for your holy support to crush the rule of the devil Fidel. They need your help. Mother and child look to you for help, Jesus in his infinite power and glory needs your help. Fighting beside him you cannot fail. America will give you guns. America will give you guns to fight. Pray that the day will be soon, and it shall dawn. Praise Jesus. Praise the holy mother. Praise our father for this day of reckoning

that will not be long. Holy, holy, holy day. It will not
be long. It will not be long. I will talk to you again
tomorrow.

(*Pause*)

(JAKE *enters.*)

JAKE: Why'd you say that about America?

MIGUEL: But America help us. They help the rebels.

JAKE: Yeah, I know that, you know that, even the people over there, they know it, but we can't say it.

MIGUEL: No?

JAKE: No way. We can't say America is behind this.

MIGUEL: But everyday they drop guns, and food, and
medicine...

JAKE: Right. But we can't say that.

MIGUEL: The speech was good, okay?

JAKE: The speech was okay. Too much about Jesus
and the holy virgin.

MIGUEL: I thought it was a nice touch.

JAKE: Too strong. Too religious.

MIGUEL: I am religious.

JAKE: I don't know, it just felt too much. I gotta say
this, Miguel, this is my gut reaction.

MIGUEL: Otherwise it's okay.

JAKE: It was very good, Miguel. Next time it will be
even better.

MIGUEL: Jake, I no learning very fast.

JAKE: Miguel, I don't have all the answers either.

MIGUEL: Jake, you teach me, I make you proud of me.

JAKE: (*Gamely, struggling with pronunciation.*) Aprendamos juntos. We learn together.

MIGUEL: Yes, we learn together. But, Jake, it's aprendemos juntos.

JAKE: (*Still struggling.*) Aprendamos juntos.

MIGUEL: (*Patting him on the shoulder.*) You'll get it.

(*Lights dim.*)

Scene Ten

(*Bay of Pigs. Cinder blocks, bags of cement.* CASTRO *and* DUQUE *sit on cinder blocks, smoking.*)

CASTRO: I used to go fishing near here. Play softball, basketball. Read, in the evenings. It's nice here.

DUQUE: No mosquitos.

CASTRO: People will come from all over to my resort, this Cuban resort. Felix, it looks good.

DUQUE: Thank you, we're going to build our own Miami Beach, right here.

CASTRO: Which bungalow is mine?

DUQUE: The big one, Number 33.

CASTRO: You know, this place used to be a shitpond, a real shitpond. But today, bungalows and highway and televison and barbeque pit.

DUQUE: Wall-to-wall carpeting. Wood paneling...

CASTRO: Pool. No, two pools...

DUQUE: Beds...

CASTRO: Big beds, with fluffy pillows...

DUQUE: Golf course...

CASTRO: No, I hate golf.

DUQUE: All this work. How long you think it will be here?

CASTRO: I don't know. You make something here, the Yankees, they want to take it away. Mr. Kennedy. Good-looking man, nice hair, nice wife, nice kids, but he doesn't know what we do here. I bring electricity to this swamp. (*Pause*) Hey Felix, you shouldn't cut your beard, you know? Bardudos are the symbol of the revolution. Everyone in the movement have a beard but you, it doesn't belong to you, it belongs to the revolution.

DUQUE: Well, it's too hot. My kids didn't recognize me, and besides, I don't like making love with a beard. I'm not a soldier, I'm a builder. Look, I get things done. We're putting up twelve-foot lights over there, people can see anyone going in, going out. Forty-three bungalows on the Bay of Pigs. All part of the triumph of the revolution.

(*Pause.* TWO SMALL BOYS *run on.*)

DUQUE: Hey, hey, my little friends, where are you going?

CHILD: Looking for people to play.

CASTRO: What do you play?

CHILD: Cubans and Yankee invaders. But nobody want to be Yankee, cause they always lose.

CASTRO: You hear that, Felix, they always lose.

(*They laugh.*)

Hey my friend, you know how to play baseball?

CHILD: No, sir.

CASTRO: I have a ball here. (*Pulls out baseball.*) See this? This is a big-league ball, huh?

CHILD: Yes.

CASTRO: I pitch it to you, you throw it back. We'll start with that.

CHILD: All right.

CASTRO: You live here?

CHILD: Oh yes.

CASTRO: It's very pretty now.

CHILD: Yes.

CASTRO: Now you throw the ball back.

CHILD: Here.

CASTRO: Now I throw.

CHILD: I got it.

CASTRO: I want you to keep that baseball, all right?

CHILD: Thank you.

CASTRO: You tell them Fidel gives you this ball. Fidel, hero of the revolution, leader of the people, you tell them you played catch with Fidel. You tell your parents it was just sunset and the sky was red and we played catch. Go now. Go play.

(*The* CHILDREN *run off.*)

CASTRO: They'll be here soon, Felix, the Americans, they'll be here. I don't know where, but they'll come.

(*Lights fade down on stage.*)

Scene Eleven

(*Up on* JAKE *to the side.*)

JAKE: In November, 1960, Jack Kennedy won the presidential election by only 100,000 votes. I voted for Nixon, personal contact has always gone a long way for me. The next month while I continued training rebels under an active volcano, the President-elect was informed of the plan devised by Central Intelligence for the overthrow of Fidel Castro. Kennedy approved the plan and a tentative date was set. The plan stated that its assessments were based on third-hand reports, and an understanding that a large underground force in Cuba would rise up on the first days of the invasion.

We are three weeks away from the invasion. I am on a destroyer to drop Miguel off at the beaches to begin transmission of propaganda. I'm going to do something good. Something good for America. I'm going back to Cuba.

(*The deck of a destroyer.* JAKE, MIGUEL.)

JAKE: Miguel, you look green.

MIGUEL: I turning green, yes.

JAKE: What, you don't like boats?

MIGUEL: I'll be happier on the beach. Thank you for the women, Jake.

JAKE: Women, what women? (*He looks around.*)

MIGUEL: Back at the base. Thank you for getting the whores for all of us.

JAKE: No problem, Miguel.

MIGUEL: Many of the people, the freedom fighters like myself, were horny, you know? People were looking at animals with lust. We are training to liberate Cuba, yes. But all the time, all day and night all we talk about is women. All we think about is whores, huh? Then the whores come and I thank you, Jake. Now I feel good. I can go in the boat back to Cuba and give out the guns and talk on the radio and give the money and get the people ready for the day of liberation.

JAKE: I'm glad you feel better.

MIGUEL: Lust for animals is a serious sin, Jake. We all know this, but the men lust anyway, till the whores come.

JAKE: Well, you can thank the United States government for the women, not me.

(*Pause*)

MIGUEL: See, off there. There's the beaches of Cuba. I land there tonight, and I am back in Cuba. Back home. Thank you for the whores, Jake.

JAKE: Hey, it's okay, Miguel. I'm glad I could help out.

MIGUEL: Things were very ... what?

JAKE: Tense?

MIGUEL: No.

JAKE: Uh, what do you want to say?

MIGUEL: I guess tense. Things were tense without the women. We could not work. I'm a religious person, but I like women. We all pray, but soon we pray to the virgin to bring us women. Who knows, maybe I go back to Cuba and die, maybe Castro he finds me and puts me in prison and I die, without you know, this tenseness going away.

JAKE: Miguel, all four years I was in high school I felt like that.

MIGUEL: They give you whores?

JAKE: No, didn't work like that.

MIGUEL: One woman I saw, she does things with her, you know, her thing. I see her smoke a cigarette with her thing, huh, Jake? She take a bottle of Coca-Cola and a straw. She put the straw up her thing, the Coca-Cola go up the straw into her thing, then back down the straw back into the bottle. She put her legs way over her head and walk upside down on her feet, then her hands. Then she bend back and touch her rear end with her face, then she stand on a chair and with one foot in the air do something with the cigarette. Then she sing and spread her legs and stand on the chair on her hands, then she on one hand and one foot put the other foot around her arm and touch her nose. Then she take cigarette between toes and take it out of mouth with other foot while arms wrapped around chair legs and she stand on her head under chair with legs up in the air. Then she take both her feet in her hands and over the chair reaches up and lifts chair with her tongue at the same time she opens her thing and puts head inside. She was very popular woman. But this was before. Under Batista.

JAKE: Miguel, you saw this woman do these things?

MIGUEL: Yes, and I say thank you, Jake and thank you government of United States for the women.

(COMMANDER TYLER *comes over.*)

TYLER: Well, Miguel, you ready to go?

MIGUEL: Yes.

TYLER: You do us proud, son. You get those rebels ready for the invasion.

MIGUEL: I will.

TYLER: You trained these men, Jake?

JAKE: I taught them to be broadcasters.

MIGUEL: He teach me to talk on the radio, to give money, to train others.

TYLER: Jake, I have complete confidence in these people. This operation is gonna go so smooth, gonna look like a fucking folk festival. Miguel, just remember, you do your job. Then in three weeks when the first shot is fired, when your buddies hit the beaches, every town, every province is gonna rise up against old Fidel. They'll grab their rifles and their grenades and whatever they got and whip shit into lather. Just remember that, Miguel, when you land on that beach tonight.

MIGUEL: I will.

JAKE: Miguel, be careful.

MIGUEL: Jake, when Fidel come everyone cheers and rushes into the street. I too was there cheering with them. Then soon people come to my house, take my brother to jail. My brother is a painter, so they take him to jail. The writers, the painters, the teachers, the musicians, they take to jail. They take my uncle's farm and they put him in jail. They make his farm into some—I don't know, a lot of people we never know move there. Then people come to the house and start executions. The writers are executed, the teachers, the people with money. They are enemies of Fidel, so they are executed. They are pushed against the wall and shot. So I leave Cuba, I leave everything I have. But I come back now and if I can cut off Castro's balls, huh? Then I go to church and pray he burns forever.

TYLER: Your boat is ready to go, son.

(*They exit.* JAKE *looks out.* TYLER *comes back. A jet screams across overhead.*)

TYLER: I smell combat, Jake. I smell a war here.

JAKE: Uh huh.

TYLER: Jake, I got transport over to the Essex. A little party there tonight. Celebrate the 103,000th jet landing on the Essex. We cut a cake, take a few photos for every thousandth landing. And we like our cake.

JAKE: Wouldn't miss it for the world, Commander.

TYLER: Yes, sir, I smell smoke, and where there's smoke...

JAKE: Yeah.

TYLER: I'm a motherfucker, Jake. I like the part where he said he'd cut off Castro's balls, like that kind of motherfuck talk.

JAKE: Yeah. (*He looks out.*) So this is Cuba.

TYLER: That's it.

(*Lights dim.*)

End of Act One

ACT TWO

Scene One

JAKE: When my sister was just fourteen, she thought she might have fallen in love. There was this boy, Ramon. He wanted to marry her, he said. Marry her and raise a family and be a doctor in America. If that wasn't possible, he was willing to share the wealth of Cuba. We've just been to a dance at the Tropicana. And this is Havana, April 1939.

(LINDA *in dress runs on.*)

JAKE: Linda, we gotta go.

LINDA: Not yet.

JAKE: Dad said you're supposed to take me back to the Hotel.

LINDA: Listen, Jake, I'm gonna meet Ramon here so why don't you go back.

JAKE: But it's night time.

LINDA: So?

JAKE: This is a foreign country. I don't even speak Spanish.

LINDA: You'll be all right.

JAKE: Dad said after that dance you're supposed to walk me back.

LINDA: Jake, don't be a jerk, just go by yourself.

JAKE: But Dad said after that dance you're supposed to walk me back.

LINDA: Look, just tell him I walked you back.

JAKE: But you didn't, that would be lying. I would have to lie to Dad.

LINDA: That's not a lie, look I'll walk you to the corner and you'll go the rest of the way.

JAKE: But...

LINDA: Jake you see this fist? It's gonna connect with your little face in a second if you don't disappear.

JAKE: What's so great about this Ramon guy?

LINDA: Ramon is ... he's real romantic. He dances like a dream, he says things like in the movies.

JAKE: Linda, I don't wanna go home by myself and I AM NOT GOING TO LIE TO DAD.

LINDA: Jake, here he comes go, get lost or you are gonna be smashed in the morning by me. Okay. You asked for it. (*She pulls his nose.*)

(JAKE *starts to go.*)

LINDA: And don't start crying or anything. And don't say anything to Dad.

(JAKE *moves to the side of the stage.*)

JAKE: Of course I didn't go back. I watched from behind a post and listened to what happened. Maybe that was wrong, but what the hell, I was ten years old.

(RAMON *enters.*)

(RAMON'S GRANDMOTHER *sits upstage, dressed in black.*)

RAMON: Oh, Linda.

LINDA: Ramon.

RAMON: I have been looking for you.

LINDA: I was out here looking at the stars and the moon, and listening to the waves, feeling the canopy of the heavens about my shoulders.

RAMON: Linda, did you make that up?

LINDA: Yes, Ramon. Who is that woman over there?

RAMON: That is my grandmother.

LINDA: Ramon, you brought your grandmother?

RAMON: She is here to protect your honor, it is a custom.

LINDA: That's sweet.

RAMON: I love you, Linda.

LINDA: Ramon, your grandmother is sitting right over there.

RAMON: She doesn't listen to us.

LINDA: Oh, yeah, I bet she doesn't. Ramon, you look like you want to kiss me, and if you try with your grandmother watching over us, I am gonna scream, and then both your parents and mine are going to be upset.

RAMON: You look like a real American movie star.

LINDA: You talk this way, it has no effect. I can't let you kiss me, I can't.

RAMON: You want to live with me in Cuba?

LINDA: No, Ramon, I got to go back to New Jersey and finish high school.

RAMON: You can't.

LINDA: I have to.

RAMON: Next summer, you come back to Cuba, and we get married.

LINDA: No, I'm going to finish high school. I can't get married, I'm trying out for band this year.

RAMON: Band?

LINDA: I play clarinet. I take lessons with Mr. Hellman after school on Wednesdays.

RAMON: You see all this, this land, this beach, it belongs to my family, then to me, I am the oldest so, so really it belongs to me. We are very rich, Linda, in Cuba everyone respects the rich, so many poor, they all look up to the rich, and that is me, and you be rich too, you marry me, see?

LINDA: I can't say yes.

RAMON: Cuba is a paradise, yes?

LINDA: It's awful swell and its so romantic, you're very romantic, but I don't live here, I don't think like you, Cuba and America are two different places.

RAMON: They are not so different, we both have the same needs.

LINDA: Look, next summer Dad is taking me and Jake to Maine, maybe Canada and so you see, Ramon, I'm probably not going to see you again, but see, you can write letters if you want.

RAMON: I must kiss you, or I'm going to explode.

LINDA: I'm gonna tell you something and you gotta try and understand. I love you, Ramon.

RAMON: I know.

LINDA: But if I kiss you once it's not gonna stop there and there is no way that can happen 'cause I can't get married this year.

RAMON: I understand, Linda.

LINDA: I thought you said she was here to protect my honor.

(They kiss quickly. YOUNG JAKE *enters.)*

JAKE: Hi.

LINDA: Jake, you're supposed to be in bed, you jerk.

JAKE: I saw you kiss, but it's okay because the old lady is asleep I think. Hi, Ramon.

RAMON: Hello, Jake.

JAKE: You growing a moustache?

RAMON: Yes.

JAKE: Don't he look like Clark Gable, Linda?

LINDA: Am-scray Jake, you little...

JAKE: You want to go swimming tomorrow, Ramon?

RAMON: Maybe

JAKE: Okey doke.

LINDA: I'm gonna murder you, Jake.

RAMON: Here is a dollar, Jake, now I'm going to walk Linda back to her room and you don't tell anyone you saw us.

JAKE: I can't do that, Ramon.

RAMON: Linda, come with me.

(They start to exit.)

JAKE: Hey, what am I supposed to do?

LINDA: Drop dead.

*(*RAMON *and* LINDA *exit.)*

JAKE: Our relationship was established even at that tender age. I always thought of Cuba as a place to fall in love, well, maybe seduced is a better word. It was night and there was water and strings of lights. After we dropped Miguel off I went to a party on the aircraft carrier and I ate cake and drank beer and told dirty jokes but all the time I wanted to go out on the deck and look at Cuba.

(*Jet screams overhead.* JAKE *looks up.*)

Scene Two

(*Lights up on two areas.* MIGUEL *at radio post,* JAKE *in communications tent.*)

MIGUEL: Jake, Jake.

JAKE: Yes, Miguel.

MIGUEL: It's me Miguel.

JAKE: I know.

MIGUEL: I'm talking from Cuba.

JAKE: Go ahead.

MIGUEL: It is night. It is very quiet. I sleep with the family that knows my family. I tell them what we talk about, about Fidel, about the day the rebels land for liberation. But I am not sure they will all fight with us on the day of liberation.

JAKE: Go on, Miguel.

MIGUEL: Jake, where are all the supplies?

JAKE: They're supposed to be dropped off at the point we discussed.

MIGUEL: I get no supplies. I get nothing for two weeks now. If the planes come, they miss and drop them into the ocean.

JAKE: I'll check this out for you, Miguel.

MIGUEL: One time, they drop money, Cuban money you print up, but the colors are wrong. You print up the money for me, but it's the wrong colors, it's not good, you know?

JAKE: Miguel, I ... I don't know what to say. I'll look into this. You keep up the good work.

MIGUEL: Good work don't mean anything, no one talks to me. They are so afraid, everyone is in jail. Jake, there is no underground here, you know?

JAKE: What? What did you say, Miguel?

MIGUEL: But we will do okay. We will fight and win, and free Cuba.

JAKE: Miguel ... there's got to be ... I mean, they told us about these people ... our intelligence reports...

MIGUEL: There is no one, Jake. No one here. They are all in jail.

JAKE: Miguel, oh God, be careful. I'll talk to the people here. I swear.

MIGUEL: You are the only person talks to me, Jake. So can I talk to you?

JAKE: Sure, Miguel.

MIGUEL: Then you will hear from me. I will be here and I will radio you. Goodnight.

JAKE: Goodnight.

MIGUEL: Jake?

JAKE: Yes?

MIGUEL: What was the movie this week?

JAKE: *Gigi* with Leslie Caron, Maurice Chevalier, Louis Jourdan, uh, uh...

MIGUEL: And Hermione Gingold.

JAKE: Right.

MIGUEL: Thank you Jake.

(*Lights out on* MIGUEL. JAKE *looks at his radio, lights dim on him.*)

JAKE: Goodnight, Miguel.

Scene Three

(LINDA *at table in bar. Miami.* RODGER *brings drinks over.*)

LINDA: I have to go.

RODGER: Not yet, just one more drink. (*He toasts.*)

LINDA: Thank you.

RODGER: You know, it's funny Linda. Everybody wants to dress just like Jackie. It's the damnedest thing, but it's true. She's wearing one of those dresses designed by some French designer, and she gets her picture in the paper planting some baby tree in the playground of Calvin Coolidge Junior High or something and the very next day everybody's running out, trying to get a dress like Jackie wore. People want to dress like her and talk like her, and just be like her, you know? It's the damndest thing.

LINDA: You don't approve.

RODGER: Oh no, Linda, it isn't that. It's just funny. Now Jack, he's okay, people like Jack, he's young, he's fresh, but they love Jackie. People say it's her oughta be running the country.

LINDA: You could do worse.

RODGER: I'll tell her you said so.

LINDA: Thanks.

RODGER: She enjoys your pieces, she really does. She reads the stuff you write and thinks this is tough, this is ballsy, pardon my French, but it is. It's got guts. It's on the move and its progress. It reads like she talks.

LINDA: Thanks. You know, Rodger, it's amazing how quickly you found me. You people from the White House, I mean. I couldn't believe it when you called me at my hotel today. I didn't think anyone knew I was here, but son of a gun if you didn't find me.

RODGER: That's because we've had our eye on you. The way you operate, your style.

LINDA: Well, that's nice. You know what I'm doing here, Rodger, in Miami. I know you know, but I'll tell you anyway, because I'm so gutsy. I was talking to the head of the Cuban exile government. He was very open and eager to talk to me, even after I told him I work for *Time* magazine. He said that the United States Navy was gonna escort these Cuban rebels that don't exist right up to the beaches, and that he was promised Air Force fighters for support. I asked him wasn't it odd that representatives of our government should conduct business of an extremely sensitive nature in such a public place as the Century Club here in Miami, and he said no, it didn't seem odd to him. He told me that everyone knew the United States was behind the invasion of Cuba.

(*Pause*)

RODGER: Well Linda, I'm here to tell you that you could do more for your country.

LINDA: What do you mean?

RODGER: You could do more by working for Jackie.

LINDA: I don't understand.

RODGER: You're great at what you do, why don't you do it at the White House. Be Jackie's press secretary.

LINDA: Well, I'm flattered you think I could do something for my country.

RODGER: We'd like you to start right away. Of course, but you'd have to leave Time-Life. (*Pause*) I hope you'll think about this offer.

LINDA: Well, I'm thinking about it right now. Why don't we order dinner?

RODGER: All right.

(*Lights dim.*)

Scene Four

(*CIA office.* TANNER, JAKE, RODGER, BOB.)

TANNER: Afternoon everybody. Bob, Rodger, Jake. How is Guatemala?

JAKE: Fine.

(*Pause*)

TANNER: Rodger, would you take a memo. I want these underground anti-Castro infiltrators told that when they go out in the field to tie a grenade to their upper thigh, and that if they are captured they are to escape possible confession through torture by asking to go the bathroom and then blowing themselves up.

RODGER: You want them to blow themselves up testicles first?

TANNER: I would like a memo to that effect. Bob?

BOB: Great news, Tom. OSD has talked with the boss at Coca-Cola. They feel—

JAKE: Sir...

TANNER: Yes, Jake?

JAKE: I think it's kind of a silly recommendation. It's possible it will be seen as an insult, and I just think it's crazy.

TANNER: You think it's crazy, Rodger?

RODGER: Well, yes, it is a little.

TANNER: Okay, fine, forget it. No, type it up anyway, but don't send it out yet.

BOB: As I was saying. They feel they could have the Havana bottling plant operational by May 15th.

JAKE: Mr. Tanner, sir, I've trained these rebels, I've started boating them into Cuba, and they are very,

very serious about their country, about their com-
mitment to their country, but there seems to be some
lack of communication between us down in Guatemala and Nicaragua, and up here in Washington. I
don't know what to tell these people, who get a little
pissed off about receiving these orders and, you
know, and not receiving their shipments.

TANNER: Jake, it's taken care of.

JAKE: Sir...I have information to the effect...

TANNER: Jake, it's taken care of.

JAKE: ...all pockets of resistance.

TANNER: When these freedom fighters hit the
beaches, the second wave will be a provisional government, the government that we have recognized
now in exile in Miami. This government will ask for
American air support and military assistance. And
they will get it.

JAKE: You're saying Americans will be involved.
What are we talking about here?

TANNER: I'm saying that a friendly govenment of the
Western hemisphere, a government of true Cuba,
will ask for American military support and bat-
tleships and planes could come in there and kick shit
and Jake, I resent these questions and I appreciate
your concern but you make me angry and really it's
none of your fucking business, all right?

JAKE: All right. That's what's going to happen?

TANNER: We have every reason to believe Kennedy
will come around to our way of thinking. Really,
Jake, we have no time to be consulting Cubans on
this thing. We've already planned and we're going to
succeed and you can go back to the swamps and keep
quiet. It is a courtesy that you are here ... it is a favor
on my behalf. So if you will please sit down, we can
proceed.

(*Pause*)

BOB: I'm sure it was an oversight on his part, Tom.

TANNER: Yes. Well. That is probably what it was. Rodger, will you type up that memo?

RODGER: Right away, sir.

TANNER: Jake, remember who you're talking to.

JAKE: I do.

TANNER: Jake, we don't have time for this, we really don't. I want people on those beaches in about two weeks, and I am going to tell Jack Kennedy that, to his face, and you know what? They'll be there, kicking Castro's behind in two weeks.

JAKE: I'm glad you set me straight sir.

TANNER: Yes.

JAKE: We are liberating Cuba after all.

TANNER: Yes.

JAKE: Just so I know. Just so I can tell the Cubans I work with.

TANNER: Very good.

JAKE: Yeah.

TANNER: Let me explain one thing, Jake. You tell things to these Cubans, it is all over town. It could be in the paper. It could be in *Time* magazine, I could read embarrassing information in *Time* magazine and we are compromised, aren't we, Jake?

JAKE: Yes, sir.

TANNER: And you could be on the boats on the day of the invasion. I know that's where you'll want to be. Right up front. Right in on the game, Jake. Take it from me, it'll be some show. And you'll be right there, Jake. Then you'll come back here, back to my office and tell me all about it, right?

JAKE: All right, sir. I'll do that.

TANNER: Fine, Jake. And if we invade New Zealand, I'll consult you early on, in the planning stages. (*He smiles.*) Goodbye, Jake.

JAKE: Goodbye. (*He exits.*)

TANNER: Now let's move one.

(*Lights dim.*)

Scene Five

(*Late at night, lights up on* JAKE *in one area.*)

(*Phone rings. Lights up on another area.* NIXON *enters, in bathrobe.*)

JAKE: Hello, Mr. Nixon.

NIXON: Who is this?

JAKE: This is Jake. Jake Seward.

NIXON: Jake?

JAKE: Caracas. I was with you in Caracas, the riot with the students.

NIXON: Oh, Jake Seward. You were with the embassy, right?

JAKE: Right. Listen, I'm sorry you lost the election, sir. Only 100,000 votes, that's very very close. And I voted for you, sir. If I could I would have voted twice.

NIXON: Thank you, Jake. Well, we tried.

JAKE: I'm sorry it's so late, sir, I know you're busy. I hope I didn't take you away from some important work.

NIXON: No, no, just having some hot chocolate, reading, keeping up to date on world affairs, that kind of thing.

JAKE: I hope the weather's nice, it's a little cold here in Washington...

NIXON: Now Jake, you didn't call me up to talk about the weather.

JAKE: No, sir.

NIXON: Well, what is it Jake?

JAKE: I need ... I guess I want some advice.

NIXON: I put in a word for you, Jake. Maybe you didn't know that but I did. Richard Nixon doesn't forget. Never forget who your friends are, Jake. Or your enemies.

JAKE: Yes, sir, I thought you might have put in a word. I'm sorta involved with the Cuba thing.

NIXON: Nasty subject, Jake. When Fidel came to New York I knew we were gonna have trouble. I knew he was Commie from the word go. Bright, intelligent, but Red. Red as a beet. And let me tell you, Jake, I can sniff out a Commie like nobody's business. Now Cuba, that's a problem that should be eradicated from the Western hemisphere immediately.

JAKE: It's not ... our ... my involvement is not moving forward as planned. I'm not sure how I can talk to you about this.

NIXON: Don't worry, Jake. I've been keeping tabs on this situation, I still have some contacts at State, I've been briefed.

JAKE: I ... I'm just afraid some people might get left on the beaches, sir, Cubans, and the people just haven't rallied like ... what we need. The rebel underground is above ground, they're in jail.

NIXON: That's not good, Jake, not good at all.

JAKE: I know it's not good, but what can I do sir? I don't call the shots, my hands are kinda tied.

NIXON: I know what that's like Jake. Remember I was Vice-President. Not that I didn't try to make something of it.

JAKE: Yes, sir.

NIXON: You want my advice, Jake?

JAKE: Sir.

NIXON: Don't back down, do what you believe is right. What you know to be right with the information available. You do that and you'll sleep better at night knowing you did your best. You know, this whole thing was originally my plan. But I have the impression that the original scenario has been corrupted, watered down by a bunch of East Coast, Ivy League, Liberal professors who never saw a day of action. I was in the Navy, Jake, and I know how to take command. Jake, you just go in and say your piece and don't back down.

JAKE: Thank you, Mr. Vice-President.

NIXON: Not anymore, Jake. Mr. Nixon is fine.

JAKE: Thank you, Mr. Nixon. Give my best to Pat.

NIXON: I will. How's the nose by the way?

JAKE: Fine, it was just a flesh wound.

NIXON: Jake. Thank you for calling and talking to me. Thank you.

JAKE: Sure.

NIXON: I just wanted ... well, goodnight Jake. Goodnight.

(*Lights dim.*)

Scene Six

(*Lights up on store.*)

LINDA: Jake, over here. Try this jacket.

JAKE: I like this one.

LINDA: The plaid. God, you got taste in your mouth.

JAKE: I like this jacket.

LINDA: Don't worry. I'm going to make you look great. Real swank. A real Kennedy.

JAKE: I don't want to ... look like...

LINDA: Shut up already.

JAKE: Hey Linda, guess what?

LINDA: What?

JAKE: We're going to invade Cuba.

LINDA: Yeah?

JAKE: You know, I mean everybody knows, but if you want confirmation...

LINDA: You don't want to be saying this to me, Jake.

JAKE: I thought...

LINDA: You tell me anything, they are gonna find who said things and then it's not going to be a slap on the hand and besides I know everything already, only we were told to just put it away.

JAKE: Forget about it?

LINDA: File it and forget it. We had it all down and we were told to keep quiet. Besides...

JAKE: What?

LINDA: Well, I might be working for them so it was better not to cause any grief.

JAKE: Work for who?

LINDA: Your bosses, the White House. I'm going to work for the President.

JAKE: For Kennedy.

LINDA: Well, for Mrs. Kennedy, for Jackie. So they asked me for a little favor, and they asked Time-Life for a bigger favor and hey, we're all good patriotic Americans, right? We're asked a favor by the President to shut up. In the interest of national security. So don't say anything more to me, Jake. How do you know they don't have people following you right now? How do you know?

JAKE: I don't.

LINDA: That's right, you don't. You don't know if they listen in on your phone calls, which they do. They played me a couple. Surprise, Jake.

JAKE: Trick or treat.

LINDA: I'm gonna work for them, you think I don't have to go through some big deal security clearance? Wake up, Jake. You're a risk.

JAKE: So you got a job with Jackie.

LINDA: Mrs. Kennedy is great. We could use some class around here. Kennedy makes you feel like this country is goddamn alive (*Pause*) I thought you said you had more taste than Mamie Eisenhower. If I left you alone you'd dress like her.

JAKE: Mamie Eisenhower has become a very close friend of mine, so please...

LINDA: Look, Jake, I only got a certain amount of time to shop with you. In two weeks this thing, it'll be over and done with. Like they told me, file it and forget it.

JAKE: You're right, Linda. Next week Castro will be bulldozing a couple hundred Cubans off the beach. And Jack and Jackie will give a dinner party and I'm sure there'll be plenty of hot shots for you to rub elbows with.

LINDA: Are you finished, Jake? You got your gripes, you forget it.

JAKE: Isn't anybody telling the President ... doesn't anybody say, "Jack, hey guy, there's no way this thing is going to work."

LINDA: I happen to know that Kennedy still can say no, but what are we going to do with fifteen hundred freedom fighters armed and waiting in landing craft? Let them loose in Central Park? Give a day on us at Disneyland? It's their country. If they want to fight, let them fight.

JAKE: Linda, I am taken aback by this sudden humanitarian concern you have acquired.

LINDA: I'm just being realistic, Jake. Just like everybody else.

JAKE: I think I'll take the plaid. (*He starts to exit.*)

LINDA: Say hello to the FBI agents by the door on your way out.

JAKE: (*He stops.*) Linda, I need to...

LINDA: Jake, you dumb jerk. For once in your life be smart, and just keep your mouth shut. Send me a postcard from Havana. (*She smiles.*)

JAKE: Right, right.

(*Lights dim.*)

Scene Seven

(*Lights up on another section of the stage.* LARRY *enters.*)

LARRY: Jake?

JAKE: Yes.

LARRY: I'm Larry, Larry Peters.

(*They shake hands.*)

LARRY: I'm glad we could talk.

JAKE: Sure, I...

LARRY: I appreciate your courage in ... you know, coming forward with this information.

JAKE: Look...

LARRY: Let me say something here, Jake, okay? Not a lot of people, no one I know of, would do what you're doing. And we know, you and I know, what is going on. What is happening. I've been down to Miami, I've talked to people down there, I've even contacted my sources in the State Department. And one thing I keep hearing, it just won't work, you know? It's not going to happen. Our force is ill-supplied, ill-trained, I mean it's a joke basically. A joke that could have international...

JAKE: Mr. Peters, I felt that ... I feel that it is important that people understand why we ... I mean originally, I became involved in this operation because of the necessity.

LARRY: Sure, sure, I know. Really.

JAKE: I trained those people, Mr. Peters. And I would not say that they are unwilling to go and ... they're willing to die there. They're willing to die to liberate their country, and they believe in what they're doing, and I just wanted to make that clear. I have some important material with me. Memos, and ... you could use that, right? I mean I believe that the idea behind is...

LARRY: I know what's going to happen, I got that much. But not the fine points, but not enough to put it on the front page and have Jack Kennedy open the paper in the morning and say "Holy shit, Mr. and Mrs. Front Porch in Boise, Idaho, see what a mess we've made and I'm going to call this thing off before it blows up in my face."

JAKE: Um, exactly.

LARRY: So I need you to confirm, as a source. Your name is never going to be mentioned, understand? You'll be mentioned as a source.

JAKE: (*He pulls out manila folder.*) It's called Operation Pluto. You can open this. The U.S. Navy will escort this invasion force to the coast off the Bay of Pigs, the landing being at...

(RODGER *enters.*)

RODGER: Hello, Jake.

JAKE: This is a set up. You fuckers set me up.

RODGER: You set yourself up.

JAKE: This is supposed to be a reporter from the...

RODGER: He is what he says he is. What the fuck did you intend to do, Jake? What? Pulling this shit here. Larry called us after you called him. Incredibly stupid twisted logic you're thinking, Jake. This thing is going to happen, Jake. What did I say to you early on, Jake? Can you live with a hostile Communist government ninety miles off from here? We've got thousands of people involved, millions spent, the machinery is in motion and it's not going to stop. But who the fuck do you figure you are, Jake?

JAKE: You know why I'm doing this, Rodger.

RODGER: Those boats are on their way, fellah. The Cubans will see those boats on Sunday morning and that's it, and no Ivy League poly-sci major can stop it.

JAKE: You know what's happend, Rodger? You know what's going to happen? We're fucked, Rodger. We're fucked.

(*Lights dim.*)

Scene Eight

(*The beaches of the Bay of Pigs.* MIGUEL *and* TWO BRIGADE SOLDIERS *on the beach.* MIGUEL *has a wound in his right leg.*)

JORGE: We're fucked.

SECOND SOLDIER: Up to my neck in this swamp, huh? Fighting in swamps, I get on the radio, I say help us, help us, I see the American ships pull away. They pull away.

MIGUEL: I saw some planes, they just went overhead and were gone.

JORGE: I don't care if they fucking kill me.

MIGUEL: They will.

So they kill me. Three days I been without food, huh? No food, no water, people shooting at my ass, fucking shooting at my beautiful ass. Women telling me how beautiful my ass is, and Castro is shooting at my asshole. So I come to kill him, I been digging in the fucking sand a day and a half looking for water to drink, huh?

SECOND SOLDIER: We're a big threat, huh, Miguel? No water, no bullets, everybody gone, no planes to cover us...

(*Jeep pulls up with* CASTRO *and* FELIX DUQUE.)

DUQUE: Hey there, throw down your weapons.

MIGUEL: What weapons? No bullets, see, no bullets?

SECOND SOLDIER: No bullets since yesterday.

CASTRO: So you are the mercenaries of the American CIA?

MIGUEL: We are Cubans, sir.

DUQUE: Piece of shit.

CASTRO: So, the CIA leaves you here to die. Die on the beaches. So, now you know. You won't die, you are alive. You are in Cuba. You are back home. But you come home trying to kill your brother. For what? To fight for America? To fight for CIA? Where is the CIA, my friends? I don't see them here, fighting beside you. They aren't around now. They don't do shit. Maybe they tell you Fidel will push you against the wall and shoot you. They tell you I torture you. I won't. You will be punished, and you will be educated, and you will go back to work.

JORGE: (*To* JAKE, *who walks on.*) I was shot two weeks from this day.

SECOND SOLDIER: I was tried and put in prison for eight years. I then farmed an area outside of the Escambray Mountains.

MIGUEL: (*To* JAKE) I was arrested, tried, and served 18 years in various Cuban prisons. For the first five years I was in a forced labor camp working in sugar cane fields. I died shortly after my release.

(*Lights dim.*)

Scene Nine

(*Table and two chairs stage center.* JAKE *sits at one side of the table; out of the shadows comes* LINDA.)

JAKE: See this?

LINDA: What?

JAKE: I'm wearing the suit you picked out.

LINDA: Oh, yes.

JAKE: Pretty funny, right?

LINDA: Yes.

(*Pause*)

JAKE: Shows that I have some class. Doesn't it show that?

LINDA: Yeah. (*Pause*) You're in a lot of trouble, brother.

JAKE: Yeah, maybe I am. Sorry about your job.

LINDA: I thought you were smarter than this. I thought you were going to do something.

JAKE: For God, for country, and for Yale. Not necessarily in the order. Jesus, I'm scared. I'm scared of what they're going to do to me. Throw me in some hole and toss the key into the Gulf of Mexico.

LINDA: Maybe they will.

JAKE: Come see me, Linda. If you can. Come and talk to me.

LINDA: What were you thinking about? Why did you ever put yourself in this position?

JAKE: I remember we had a good time in Cuba.

LINDA: I remember nice beaches, and music, and the Tropicana Hotel, the stage show at the Tropicana. I remember Ramon and him kissing me and how good that was.

JAKE: There was a photo of us. A black-and-white snapshot. You're in a black swimsuit holding hands with a little me. I'm in white shorts and black knee socks and saddle shoes and I was smiling. I remember it was one of the best days of my life.

LINDA: The back of the photo said Havana, April 1939.

JAKE: Yes.

LINDA: I still have that photograph. Only I wasn't in a swimsuit, I was wearing a red dress with a slit up the side. And you weren't in saddle shoes and socks, you were barefoot and you were crying because you hated to have your picture taken. (*Pause*) You'll be out of here sometime, Jake. And I'll still be here, and these guys will still be running the country and Cuba will still be ninety miles away.

JAKE: I was barefoot, huh?

LINDA: And crying, you were always crying about something then. What a pain in the ass you were. Couldn't take you anywhere, I seem to recall.

JAKE: Linda ... nothing is ... I don't remember the photo right and...

(*Pause*)

LINDA: Jake, you were ten years old.

JAKE: So it was nothing special, right?

LINDA: I felt grown up in Cuba. I felt like a rich lady. I wore nice clothes and went to nightclubs. I fell in love. 'Course the country was corrupt, there was incredible poverty, people were tortured, but yeah, I had a good time. I was a kid. They made me feel special.

(*Light dim on* LINDA.)

MIGUEL: I think about how the United States left us on the beaches and I think, okay, we took the chance to liberate our country, our home from Fidel, and we lost. We tried and we lose. But on some nights I say fuck America, too.

TANNER: John Kennedy told me if this were the British government I would resign and you, being a senior civil servant, would remain. But it isn't. In our government you have to go and I have to remain.

NIXON: I told the president I would find proper legal cover and I would go in to Cuba. As far as I was concerned, Kennedy was chicken about committing. He always was chicken about committing. It was a bigger fuck-up than PT109.

RODGER: The joke they told me around Washington was "Caroline Kennedy certainly is a nice kid, but that's the last time we let her plan a Cuban invasion."

CASTRO: You know Kennedy is gone. And so is Eisenhower and Nixon and Kruschev, all are gone. But I'm still here. Fidel is still here.

JAKE: When I heard the report coming in on the radio, April 19, 1961, I looked out the window. Outside the sky was clear blue and I started to cry and I threw up. The report kept coming in all day. I just cried and threw up for three hours. I thought "How could we have been so dumb?" Then I thought if it hadn't been this time at the Bay of Pigs, it would have been somewhere else, at some other time.

(*LIGHTS DIM. Andrew sisters sing* "Rum and Coca-Cola".)

NATIVE SPEECH

BY ERIC OVERMYER

A riveting play, rich in texture and rife with allusion, which provides a chilling vision of civilization about to go belly up. Originally produced at the **Los Angeles Theater Center** in the summer of 1983. Seven males, three females, though one more of each can be used. Single interior set plus an exterior playing area.

TRANSIENTS WELCOME

BY ROSALYN DREXLER

From one of Off Off Broadway's original and most **delightfully crazed** playwrights here are three little plays that are full of her typically bizarre characters. ROOM 17C calls for two males (one playing a cockroach) and one female. LOBBY has three males and two females, and UTOPIA PARKWAY has four females and one male. All three have simple interior sets. This script also has a preface written by Newsweek theater critic Jack Kroll.

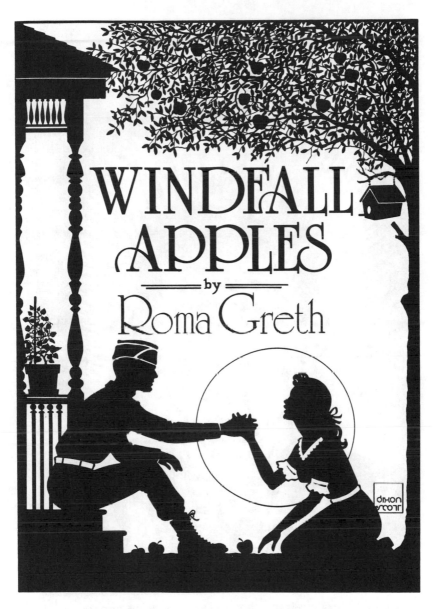

WINDFALL APPLES

by

Roma Greth

This gem of a play evokes the **days of youth and innocence** as our boys were being shipped off to World War II. This play workshopped at the **Eugene O'Neill Theater Center** in the summer of 1977, and then was produced in Manhattan at the IRT late in 1978. Three males, three females; single interior and exterior set.

BATTERY

BY DANIEL THERRIAULT

Electricity is the central metaphor and expressive image in this unusual love story which takes place in an electrical repair and systems design shop located in Chicago. Therriault has an exceptional ear for American speech patterns, and has been **compared to Sam Shepard and David Mamet for his superb use of language.** First produced in New York at St. Clement's Theater in the Spring of 1981. Two males, one female; single interior set.

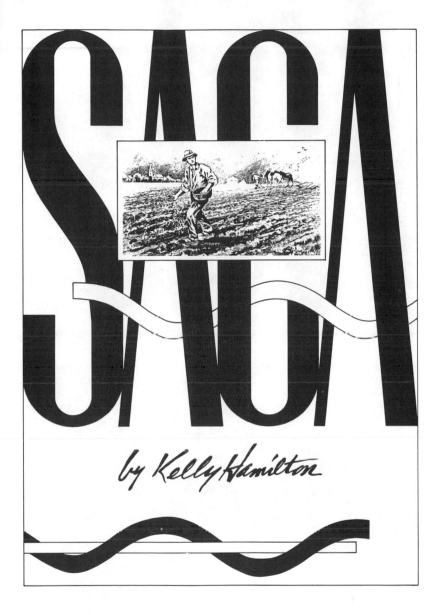

SAGA

by Kelly Hamilton

This wonderful **musical** is a history of America's pioneers as they push their way across the country. A minimum of eight males and eight females are necessary, and the show can be expanded to use many more actors. Settings can be fluid and simple or elaborate.